"BUT, We've Always Done It That Way"

Why Businesses Fail

Human Frailties Inhibiting Progress

Learning From a Microcosmic Endeavor,

A Test and Challenge for Every Business Environment

The Author:

Daniel W. Fritz is an Experienced, 'Hands-On' Business Development, Process Management Professional Specializing in: Analyzing Business Endeavors and Facilitating the Incorporation of New Processes, Programs, and Enhancements while Employing a Background of Extensive Experiences of Enhancing Social Programs in Diverse Settings.

Introduction:

This simple straight forward presentation is a challenge!! It is a challenge to any and all business leaders, CEOs and on down the management chain to find a business where the following problems have been addressed and are not prevalent and are not actively causing business corrosion, yes business corrosion. This dissertation is about the human condition and how it affects the work environment. The corporate environment can be reengineered, it can employ technology, it can conduct endless total quality management programs, but there will always be the necessity of dealing with human frailties.

This presentation is designed as a test as well as being an interactive book with an E-Mail address available for comments. I will seek to publish a second edition with responses of how other businesses are seeking to resolve the issues delineated here.

The purpose of this treatise **is not** to give a functional listing of the reasons for business failure, but being somewhat of a social psychologist/business analysis, to present the issues of the human interactions that are at work within everyday business endeavors. There have been many presentations delineating the reasons for business failures with endless dissertations concerning leadership/management styles, business dynamics etc. This presentation is not to rehash the functional reasons for business failures but to examine the potential causes for business failures from a human perspective. The Problems/Reasons and Causes delineated here are from a rather small local endeavor but the pervasive and interesting note is that the same events are happening each day in every major corporate environment. For humanity is basically the same and is known to act out just about the same way in small or large endeavors.

The purpose of this presentation is to give each business that reviews this work the chance to question the functionality of their work environment in terms of the interpersonal dynamics set forth.

This book is not about office politics although office politics are definitively a result of the human condition and can be seen emerging from the issues set forth here. (An interesting book presenting the features of office politics has been written by Ronna Lichtenberg – 'Work Would Be Great If It Weren't for the People'). This book is set forth as a discussion of personality predispositions that sorely affect the daily ongoing business environment.

It should also be noted that this presentation is from personal participation in the endeavor (business), and the good, bad, and ugly of this fact will also be seen.

Literally thousands of articles, books, magazines, and other documents have been written on the subject of business management, strengthening business endeavors etc. The purpose of writing this presentation is to share insights gained from a small town organization and **relate that the very same issues have been experienced** in every larger corporate environment, yes I would be brash and bold and state **in every** larger corporate environment. As stated initially using these examples a challenge is set forth; **prove that these events are not occurring in your business environment. All of which raises the question, if we cannot even reasonably conduct business on the minute level how are we ever to do so on the larger corporate level? I would defy the reader to show me any corporation or business wherein some if not all of the following issues are not found.**

It should also be noted that this is not a rehashing of the needs for business reengineering, for this is done quite well in such presentations as Michael Hammer and James Champy's volume 'Reengineering The Corporation'. But this is a study of human nature in all its brutal reality and how it affects business endeavors and quite often causes the downfall or weakness thereof. What is being suggested here is not just the reasons but much more importantly the causes behind these reasons. Basically **You can fire and replace employees as often as you like, but you are always inheriting human nature with its weaknesses and foibles. Yes we are talking about changing human nature, a rather difficult if not seemingly**

impossible task but the only means in which to build a better business endeavor.

A recent example of the need for such evaluations was found in a news item that appeared in September of 2012 where 2000 workers were involved in a riot in a Chinese computer parts manufacturing plant with the company describing the incident as a 'personal dispute between several employees that escalated to include thousands of people'. As a result of this riot some 40 people were taken to the hospital and a number of individuals were arrested. Now as we are aware there are situations in China where working conditions are not ideal to say the least, but this period of confrontation was described as evolving due to a "personal dispute between several employees"

To use a well known quote, "We have found the enemy and they are us!"

Reference Business:

The endeavor (business) that is the source of this treatise is a small and from an outward appearance a well presented Thrift Shop in Sullivan County NY. **Yes, a Thrift Shop of all places**, but as related previously the human and interpersonal issues found there have been seen to be identical to those in larger corporate environments, (have been there, done that and witnessed the same), sarcasm intended!. The thrift shop has more or less a dozen 'employees' a treasurer, a governing board, (President, Vice President, Secretary etc.) and two managers and a yearly income of about $63,000. Am using this Thrift Shop as a reference point because it has allowed close interaction with all individuals and a direct experiencing of the Reasons and Causes for the business issues, and as a pragmatic matter it is also where I am currently associated and am able to conduct this study.

When an individual enters the Thrift Shop they are pleasantly surprised to see a well laid out display with nicely presented goods of varying nature; clothes, household items, CDs, DVDs, records, televisions, furniture, knick knacks etc. All goods in the store are obtained through individual donations; very similar to other benevolent institutions of this nature, but if it may be stated, of a slightly higher quality. For instance clothes that are brought in are meticulously scrutinized for stains, tears, etc, and if these are found they are rejected from presentation in the store.

The revenue that is received through the sale of these goods, after deducting expenses, is given to those in financial need throughout the community when these requests are received. Western Sullivan County NY, (also known as the 'Upper Delaware') is an area that has been severely afflicted by current economic conditions. Farming and lumbering have run their course as a means of employment and the closest centers of more significant business activity is some thirty miles away and thus many individuals and families find themselves in need of both financial and practical assistance, (rent, food, clothing, furniture etc.) Some individuals and families are leaving the area, but as is quite often the case it is difficult to uproot and leave extended family and friends. There is also great fear and apprehension concerning 'the big city'. But this is a different discussion altogether.

Being a small community the individuals requesting assistance are quite often known to those associated with the Thrift Shop giving the individuals in the store an imperative for their work and activities, indeed a very positive cause for business functionality, (more will be stated later on this issue.)

Please note that in some instances issues contradict each other. This is not a mistake but represents the fact that what may be an issue for one employee may not be so for another. This of course is part of the problem of the human presence!

Personal History of Involvement:

My personal presence in this endeavor evolved very innocently. Being part Scottish in back ground, much to my wife's dismay I am rather cheap, (I like to say thrifty), and thus have been known quite often to frequent thrift shops. Since we currently live at a relatively short distance from this Thrift Shop we had quite often stopped in and made purchases accordingly. One November I noted that they were quite busy and asked if they could use some help until Christmas. Now I am sure that I stated at that time 'until Christmas' and was assigned to 'run' the store each Thursday in that time period. Interestingly in January while on vacation in St Croix received a phone call asking where we were and why we were not at the store on our appointed Thursday. Well as life evolves working in the store every Thursday became every Tuesday and Thursday. We were eventually invited to join the Board of Directors, (not a very prestigious but well intentioned group), my wife became secretary and I became one of the store managers.

Reasons, Causes, Possible Solutions, Inhibiting Factors Preventing Solution Implementation:

In the following analysis the following format will be employed. With each 'Problem' or 'Feature' being reviewed there will also be an explanation as might be useful. With this there will be at least one if not several causes delineated. This will be followed with a possible solution(s) as well as statements of the potential inhibiting factors that would prevent solution implementation. A reference will be made in each case to the implementations to the larger corporate world with a poignant question that could be answered accordingly. Scoring might also be undertaken with a suggested three points for each issue. Sincere there are thirty-three 'Problems' or 'Features' a perfect score would be a 99 thus recognizing that there is not a perfect corporation. I would suggest that any corporation with a score less than 50 should take a serious look at the daily activities and satisfaction of the employees.

The purpose of this book is to get responses and input from organizations that have found the means of addressing the issues set forth here. Would also welcome knowing of additional issues that have been found in your workplace. If a substantial collection of responses and input is forthcoming another volume will be set forth.

I can be contacted at: TheNewEndeavor@Gmail.com

Daniel W. Fritz

NOW TO THE HEART OF THE MATTER:

Problem: Fear of Technology – Example: Many of the 'employees' of the Thrift Store are afraid to use the cash register which in this case is the most basic model that is currently available. Along the same realm several times suggestion has been made to include credit card processing. This suggestion creates a very negative apprehensive response, with the argument that this is not needed in that there is a bank ATM just down the street

Cause: Obvious - Lack of any technological experience.

Possible Solution: Educate 'employees' accordingly.

Inhibiting Factors Preventing Solution Implementation: Quite a few of the 'employees' are older and have not had contact with many current technological facilities and may not be too anxious to learn. Along with this those who are knowledgeable either do not have time or in some cases patience to teach others. Many homes in the area to do not have access to high speed internet and thus do not use e-mail, real time online information etc.

Post Script - Larger Corporate Implications: This may sound quite absurd and an isolated case for a local environment, **But** the same issue has been seen in larger corporate settings as employees seek to use or in some cases avoid new technological tools, (the newest office suite, etc) . In some instances it has been recognized that it is Upper Management who has issues dealing with new technology and they find ingenious means to rely upon middle and lower managers to undertake the advanced technological endeavors. In respect to this point, in the corporate world, as is well known, there are very significant costs to the dismissal/rehiring process. **Should time be taken to train current employees, should current employees be replaced by more capable individuals, or should corporations only hire consultants who have the specific required skill sets?**

Question: Are all of your employees technologically literate, not only computer literate, but technologically literate. Is your firm seeking to embrace every possible realm of technology that is currently available?

Problem: We've always done it that way.

Cause: Inertia with a comfortable familiar style of functioning.

Possible Solution: 1) Continual encouragement of new methodologies. 2) Bring 'employees' to understand that if 'change' is not embraced it will overrun them. 3) Phase out current employees and initiate new associates.

Inhibiting Factors Preventing Solution Implementation: 1) The more that new methodologies are encouraged the greater the pushback. 2) For the majority of individuals there is a basic intrinsic fear of change. 3) In the Thrift Shop phasing out current employees is especially difficult for being a small town everyone knows everyone else and the image will be severely tarnished. Also there is not a vast pool of potential 'employees' available to join the staff.

Critical Note: Obviously change for the sake of change is not beneficial to business endeavors. All of the standard CBA (Cost Basis Analysis) etc should be extensively considered for a reorganizational endeavor.

Now since I especially enjoy railroads and such need to include the following example written by Dan McCarthy.

Saturday, March 29, 2008

"Because that's the way we've always done it!"

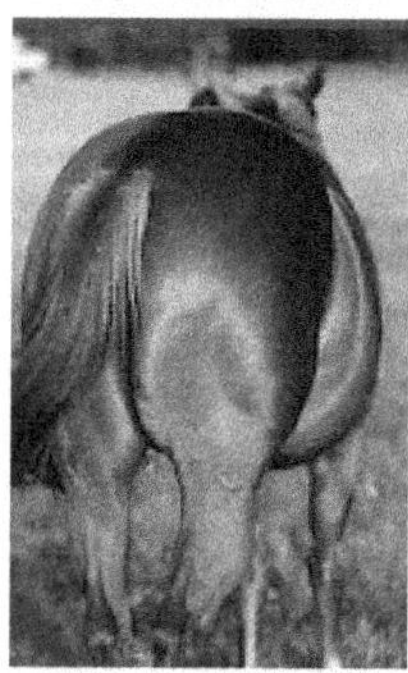

This article from the internet is in first person by Dan McCarthy.

Does the expression, "We've always done it that way!" ring any bells? The US standard railroad gauge (distance between the rails) is 4 feet, 8.5 inches. That is an exceedingly odd number. Why was that gauge used? Because that is the way they built them in England, and English expatriates built the US railroads. Why did the English build them like that?

Because the first rail lines were built by the same people who built the pre railroad tramways, and that is the gauge they used. Why did "they" use that gauge then? Because the people who built the tramways used the same jigs and tools that they used for building wagons, which used the same wheel spacing.

Okay!

Why did the wagons have that particular odd wheel spacing? Well, if they tried to use any other spacing, the wagon wheels would break on some of the old, long distance roads in England, because that's the spacing of the wheel ruts. So who built those old rutted roads? Imperial Rome built the first long distance roads in Europe (and England) for their legions. The roads have been used ever since.

And the ruts in the roads? Roman war chariots formed the initial ruts, which everyone else had to match for fear of destroying their wagon wheels. Since the chariots were made for (or by) Imperial Rome, they all had the same wheel spacing. The United States standard railroad gauge of 4 feet, 8.5 inches is derived from the original specification for an Imperial Roman war chariot.

Specifications and bureaucracies live forever. So the next time you are handed a specification and wonder what horses butt came up with it, you may be exactly right. This is because the Imperial Roman war chariots were made just wide enough to accommodate the back ends of two war-horses.

Now, the twist to the story...

There is an interesting extension to the story about railroad gauges and horses' behinds. When we see a Space Shuttle sitting on its launch pad, there are two big booster rockets attached to the sides of the main tank. These are solid rocket boosters, or SRBs. "Thiokol" makes the SRBs at their factory at Utah. The engineers who designed the SRBs might have preferred to make them a bit fatter, but the SRBs had to be shipped by train from the factory to the launch site. The railroad line from the factory happens to run through a tunnel in the mountains. The SRBs had to fit through that tunnel. The tunnel is slightly wider than the railroad track, and the railroad track is about as wide as two horses' behinds. So, a major design feature of what is arguably the world's most advanced transportation system was determined over two thousand years ago by the width of a horse's ass.

Posted by Dan McCarthy at 3/29/2008 from http://www.greatleadershipbydan.com/2008/03/because-thats-way-weve-always-done-it.html "Great Leadership"

Question: Does your business study and embrace change when applicable? Of course this also brings up the question of when and how to incorporate change, but that's your problem, not to be a part of this presentation. But, do you encourage employee innovative thinking?? Do you and your managers ask you employees weekly, if not daily if they have any new dimensions or ideas?

Problem: Head Strong Leaders

Cause: Individuals have been allowed to get into a position of control and have come to believe that they and they only own the process or business endeavor.

Possible Solution: Teach new management skills. Replace leader(s) if necessary.

Inhibiting Factors Preventing Solution Implementation: Staid managers often do not really want to learn new management skills, they are comfortable in the position they are in and are seeking all possible means to maintain that position.

Post Script – Larger Corporate Implications: Typically larger corporations develop little department fiefdoms where one individual has gained control and does not want to empower others. It takes a lot, but if the manager will not change fire them, but of course this presents the issue that the dismissed manager takes with them extensive knowledge that has not been shared with staff, are expensive to replace, require outplacement services.

For all the genuine advances made by Western manufacturers, many have failed to match the best Japanese, not through technical inadequacy, but because their people management is inferior. As shown by the obscene rewards now paid to CEOs, in America above all, Western management is still heavily top-down - though that's changing. For example, self-managed teams are among many 'human resources' initiatives being both promoted and used - but they, too, are Japanese familiars.

Edward de Bono & Robert Heller's "Thinking Managers" 08/08/2005 (Internet)

Question: Have you adequately reviewed your management functionality?? Have you allowed, no not allowed, but encouraged employees to express their opinions of their managers. Should there be timely employee reviews or management reviews??

Problem: Wishy, Washy Employees, a lot of 'Charlie Browns' who are afraid to be affective.

Cause: Individuals have not been empowered to make changes. Even in the small Thrift Shop environment the roles of the 'employees' have been well defined and they are not allowed to step out of the boundaries. If they do take initiative they are quickly and harshly reprimanded. One of the store managers of the Thrift Shop wants to maintain a predefined store structure and no one is to question or displace that structure and when someone does they are several criticized.

Possible Solution: Basically this once again depends on either retraining the managers to empower their employees, replacing the managers, or empowering the employees for shared and/or rotated management.

Inhibiting Factors Preventing Solution Implementation: In the case of the Thrift Shop some of the managers are older and seek desperately to hold onto position and are in need of the limited income that is provided for that position.

Post Script – Larger Corporate Implications: Of course the same is true in the larger corporate environment. I take the 8:17 train from Freeport, Mineola, Danberry or where ever. I am at my desk by 9:00 have lunch at 12:00 leave for the 5:20 train, in between I shuffle papers that come across my desk. What more do you want out of me?? To bring this up to date, the activity now is not paper shuffling but for many writing and responding to E-Mails. I am sure that everyone who reads this dissertation has either seen or worked with mangers who do not actually touch the work environment but spend the day creating, forwarding or responding to E-Mails.

Question: Do your employees actively suggest changes to the structure of the organization or are they just shuffling papers and/or create E-Mails?

Problem: Does Not Work or Play Well With Others. We all remember well those wonderful words from our days in elementary school; "he/she does not play well with others". There are several 'employees' in the Thrift Shop' who continually complain about how difficult it is to work with some other individual.

Cause: In the case of the Thrift Shop it is a voluntary environment so thus the workers are not required to work well with others. But this begs the question, is it possible to require individuals to work well with others? Of course not, but how do we get people to overcome their pettiness?

Possible Solution: To be very honest in the Thrift Shop not sure, we can listen, encourage better interactions but since they are volunteers no distinct pressure can brought to bear.

Inhibiting Factors Preventing Solution Implementation: It is very hard to force volunteers to change disposition. In the larger corporate environment interactive training can be provided, but social psychologists have determined that the mind set is well established by age 12. (Don't ask me for a reference for this fact.)

Post Script – Larger Corporate Implications: How much time is wasted in the corporate environment with employees complaining around the water cooler. How many problems and issues are not resolved because individuals do not want to work with each other? It is also noted that there is a distinct difference between personality conflicts and differences of opinion as to business operations. Discussion concerning business operations can be very rewarding as long as they do not become personal attacks and affronts.

Question: Do your employees work well with each other encouraging new ideas and innovations or is there an environment of constant tension?

Problem: Lack of Defined Leadership

Cause: There has been haphazard definition of leadership roles.

Possible Solution: Obvious – in the Thrift Shop periodically have the three leaders get together and discuss the open issues. But to be honest the three leaders do not really get along that well, and yes I am one of them!!

Inhibiting Factors Preventing Solution Implementation: Since this is a thrift shop with volunteer labor do we want well defined heavy handed bosses? In the corporate world do we want well defined heavy handed bosses? We do want leaders who agree with one another and present a combined vision of the current and future endeavors to be accomplished, seeking employee buy in to these goals and objectives.

Post Script – Larger Corporate Implications: Without creating great anxiety, confusion, irritation and frustration a person cannot work for more than one boss. While in the corporate world I once attended the wedding of one of my employees and watched as the poor embarrassed bride introduce me and my manager by saying; "And this is my 'real boss.'" Who is the real boss? Is the immediate manager the boss, is their manager the real boss? Are there too many bosses, do we need all these managers, have we always used this same business structure? **Question: Are your employees aware of the leadership roles, are they satisfied that the person that they work with is the qualified leader of the group or division or what have you, or do they see some higher position as the 'real' manager?**

Problem: No Vision For the Future. Unaware that other Thrift Shops are becoming prevalent in the vicinity and in fact the 'Thrift Shop Business' is becoming a franchise across the nation.

Cause: Currently a staid environment that somewhat adequately serves the community.

Possible Solution: In the case of the Thrift Shop is one needed? Should life just be allowed to run its course?

Inhibiting Factors Preventing Solution Implementation: In this case the inhibiting factor is the staid environment.

Post Script – Larger Corporate Implications: Is your business fully aware of the advancements of the competition and the worldwide competition? More pointedly in actuality does your business really, really want to be aware of the advances of other corporations.

Question: Does your corporation really want to change and embrace the future? Does your corporation have the financial and personnel resources to change and embrace the future?

Problem: Lack of Adequate Communication.

Cause: As related above the three leaders do not interrelate well, and although changes or updates are minor there is inconsistent communication to the 'employees'.

Possible Solution: Obvious – redefine and establish realms of communication between the 'managers' and the 'managers' and 'employees'.

Inhibiting Factors Preventing Solution Implementation: The three 'managers' are threatened if their realm of immediate control is challenged.

Post Script – Larger Corporate Implications: Exactly the same, each of us can relate vast numbers of occurrences where conflicting orders have been propagated by management staff. **Just ask your employees!! Do you ask your employees such questions? Shouldn't you be asking your employees such questions?**

In the corporate environment I once went to my two managers, yes I had two managers at the time, with a proposition for update and change. I was astute enough to get them in the same room at the same time and created a presentation with substantiating background facts, details, associated documents etc. The discussion quickly fell apart with the two managers arguing with each other about how to proceed with the project with the one proclaiming vehemently; "Well I am a First Vice President" and the second shouting in response, 'Well I am a Senior Vice President". With this I walked out and never was able to implement the change that would have had a positive effect on the business process.

Question: Do your employees have a real and ongoing understanding of current business objectives both on the larger corporate and on the individual department level?

Problem: Staid Community Culture

Cause: The community has lost their association with any larger metropolitan influence. Nearby towns are quickly losing their existence and thus there is no nearby supporting influence for change.

Possible Solution: None

Inhibiting Factors Preventing Solution Implementation: The community is losing innovative resources at an unprecedented rate in that other businesses are leaving town. A new business begins; finances are set forth, new store fronts created. If fortunate the business will survive for approximately six months.

Post Script – Larger Corporate Implications: It has been well established that businesses develop a staid 'Community Culture'. In one consulting association upon making a recommendation for improved business functionality was told that the firm would not even consider such an option if XYZ corporation was not doing so. It is interesting to note that XYZ corporation no longer exists.

Question: Is your corporation caught in a staid cultural environment? Now I will grant you that it is difficult to see your firm as being a business and community leader when you are in Podunk Nebraska but isn't that what you want to be?

Problem: No Vision for the future.

Cause: Staid Community Culture.

Possible Solution: Cautiously and Carefully seek to suggest innovation.

Inhibiting Factors Preventing Solution Implementation: A body at rest tends to remain at rest. The 'Thrift Shop' is a comfortable environment why should we change?

Post Script – Larger Corporate Implications: Businesses that are struggling to maintain their current corporate environment cannot extend resources for R & D and for diversification of the endeavor.

Question: Is the corporation a comfortable environment? Do we want comfortable environments? What is the balance between a comfortable environment and one that stresses innovation. Who is responsible for innovation? Does senior management embrace the potential for change? (Note a distinction here between embracing a potential for change and embracing change. Before change can be effectuated a predisposition toward accepting change has to be realized.)

Problem: What Business Are We Really In? Are we primarily here to provide clothing resources to those in need in the community, or is our task to create the best income we can so that we can financially help those in need of assistance for rent, food, medical bills etc. This debate has led to some spirited discussions and in some cases down right arguments.

Cause: There is a lack of definition of primary purpose. Over the previous years events and activities have evolved without clear statement of purpose.

Possible Solution: Redefine the Business Activity for mutual unilateral understanding.

Inhibiting Factors Preventing Solution Implementation: There are individuals with vested interest in their segment of the business

Post Script – Larger Corporate Implications: As is well known in varying forms this happens quite often in the corporate environment. We are a Brokerage Firm, our business is to sell and facilitate the trades of securities etc. However we also print, process, and mail daily confirms, monthly statements etc. Are we also in the print and distribution business? For the most of the month our distribution equipment stands idle, can we address this?

Question: Are questions constantly being raised; should we make greater use of our associated facilities? Should we venture into an associated business function?

Problem: No Sense of Ownership

Cause: Two issues contribute to this problem. The first is that only the three managers and the treasurer are paid for services to the Thrift Shop. Of course others who work there become aware of this inequity. As a nonprofit organization with very limited resources there is no stock purchase plan or any other such ownership vehicle.

Possible Solution: Have everyone receive some sort of compensation, but this would reduce the amount that is available to serve the community.

Inhibiting Factors Preventing Solution Implementation: Being a nonprofit organization with limited resources.

Post Script – Larger Corporate Implications: In the corporate world it is well known that when there is profit sharing and stock ownership programs there is much greater commitment to the organization. It is interesting to note that in the same small town of the Thrift Shop there is a supermarket that does have a stock ownership program, those employees are committed!! For reference see the section 'Stock Options and Democracy' in Robert Townsend's 'Up the Organization'.

Question: Do all of your employees have the option of stock ownership at reduced cost? Is there profit sharing across the board?

Problem: No Opportunity for Advancement

Cause: The Thrift Shop is a very small organization with very few roles and functions.

Possible Solution: For the Thrift Shop there is none that can be defined in the current structure.

Inhibiting Factors Preventing Solution Implementation: As stated above, a very small structure with limited opportunities.

Post Script – Larger Corporate Implications: Since employees seek advancement progression of position on the corporate ladder should realms of advancement be defined?

Question: Are the opportunities for advancement defined within your firm?

Problem: Working in the Thrift Shop is not a prestigious position.

Cause: In the business world Thrift Shops are generally looked upon as lower class endeavors.

Possible Solution: Not apparent.

Inhibiting Factors Preventing Solution Implementation: Nature of the business. As a reference most everyone knows the character of **Cliff Clavin**, the postal worker, know-it-all on the comedy program Cheers. Cliff so often sets forth his pride of being a man in uniform and is elated when there is for him a junior advancement in the postal system. It is indeed the epitome portrayal of the need for recognition.

Post Script – Larger Corporate Implications: Does your corporation have a defined status in the community? Have efforts been set forth to create a status in the community? Does the corporation support a little League team or some other community effort?

Question: Has you organization sought to create a definition in the community? Do you employees have a sense of identity?

Problem: No Diversity in the ongoing work activities.

Cause: Laying out the clothes and knick knacks is very mundane and repetitive. However there is diversity in the nature of items that come into the store and the individuals who come into the store.

Possible Solution: None apparent.

Inhibiting Factors Preventing Solution Implementation: The Thrift Shop activities need to be very repetitive.

Post Script – Larger Corporate Implications: Quite often in the corporate world workers in essence repeat the same function time after time, day after day.

Question: Are there opportunities for diverse work activities? Does the business environment enable or allow varied work functions?

Problem: Dealing with the Public sometimes a frustration.

Cause: For the most part the individuals who come to the store are polite and congenial and a delight to meet and talk with, but there are times when customers are demanding, demeaning, and abusive.

Possible Solution: Train those who work with the public with proper reactions to abusive customers.

Inhibiting Factors Preventing Solution Implementation: It is difficult at times to maintain a decorum when confronted with an abusive individual.

Post Script – Larger Corporate Implications: Many customers have been lost to a firm due to inappropriate employee responses. A constant refresher program should be in place for those who directly interact with the public.

Question: Is all of your staff that deal with the public of such a disposition that they can adequately deal with even the quarrelsome individuals?

Please note that before getting into the next topic I recognize that I am going where the brave dare not go but it will at least solicit some interesting response. If there is any presentation herewith that will raise hostility, aggression, and verbal if not physical threats this will do so. But it is a problem that has been prevalent in all work environments and I have yet to find a really adequate resolution.

Problem: The difference between Male and Female Management Styles and the conflicts that arise.

Cause: I am going to relate in very generalized terms and am sure that this will also create vivid responses, however; the basic issue in regards to Male and Female management styles evolve, as I comprehend, from two predominate traits. The first is that women tend to 'micromanage' whereas men tend to 'macromanage'. Of course as related above these are vast generalizations but in the Thrift Shop the other 'manager' is a women who from my perspective gets uptight about those problems that I would consider 'minor' issues and gets mad at me when I leave some of these minor issues unattended.

The second trait is that quite often a female manager will be very strong willed and in essence determined to prove herself quite often offending her associates and employees.

Possible Solution: It has long been my contention that the best management agreement would be when a man and women work together fully recognizing their different approaches to the issues at hand and agree to allow each other the freedom to take appropriate action. This of course is wishful thinking and I have never seen it occur and would be interested in learning of such instances.

Inhibiting Factors Preventing Solution Implementation: We are who we are and changing personal perspective is indeed difficult.

Post Script – Larger Corporate Implications: Who ultimately accomplishes more in the work environment??

Question: In your corporate do the male and female managers work well with each other and their respective employees or is there the constant subliminal if not blatant confrontations?

POSITVE FEATURES OF THE THRIFT SHOP

Feature: The 'Managers' and 'Officers' work in the Thrift Shop with as much commitment and enthusiasm as all others.

Reason: Has always been expected.

Consequence: 'Employees' and 'Managers' share in work and realize together the amount of effort that has to be exerted to maintain a reasonable presentation.

Post Script – Larger Corporate Implications: Previous experience has shown that in the vast corporate environment there is a distinct differentiation between the 'workers' and the 'managers' and the work undertaken accordingly. This of course leaves the workers questioning the necessity of the work undertaken by the 'managers' with either a resentment, or a striving to become 'one of them'. Employees are well aware of when the managers take the Mar lunch, and to be very truthful, I do miss the Vendor luncheons featuring significant amounts of libation.

Question: Is there the same level of commitment to the work of the firm with both the managers and employees? Is there a significant level of commitment to the firm, or is everyone there for the paycheck?

Feature: Very Small Governing Board.

Reason: Way in which established.

Consequence: Issues get addressed quickly. All attendees not only have the opportunity to express their opinions and viewpoints but are encouraged to do so. Monthly meetings are short and to the issues of current concern. The agenda is simple and straight forward, but there is a distinct opportunity for new business and the presentation of questions and concerns.

Post Script – Larger Corporate Implications: Now I could go along at great length about corporate meetings, having sat through too many of them. Never have seen a meeting where the agenda was set forth beforehand with issues outlined so that the action of the meeting was only to approve or modify the responsive proposal. I believe it is in Robert Townsend's book **'Up The Organization'** where it was proposed that all meetings should be held standing up.

Question: How distant is your governing board from your employees? Do you your employees know, or for that matter do they care who is on the governing board?

Feature: No Political Overhead

Reason: Although the Thrift Shop was created by representatives from the local Churches including Baptist, Methodist, Episcopalian, and Roman Catholic none of these Churches have had any impetuous desire to exert domineering control over the operation thereof. Just to be sure that no one is offended there are no Jewish congregations in the community, but I am sure as I can be that there are people of every religious persuasion working with us, but this is not a question that is ever raised. Anyone with a willing hand and heart is invited to participate.

Consequence: The governing board can make decisions based upon pragmatic concerns addressing the issues that might come up in the daily activities.

Post Script – Larger Corporate Implications: Of course this is diametrically opposed to the operations of any and all corporate entities. In a publically traded firm there is of course the necessity of answering to the stock holders, the board of directors, Senior Management etc. In some format or other every employee feels responsible to the 'higher authorities".

Question: How extensive is the overhead of your firm, how many different levels have to be answered?

Feature: No Annual Meeting

Reason: Never required, no sense to have one.

Consequence: No lengthy reports to prepare, no stock holders or others with vested interest to appease.

Post Script – Larger Corporate Implications: Obvious, if only this could be the case, but the SEC would never allow it. Would save a lot of time, paper, and trouble. I am sure that other implications do not have to be rendered.

Question: How cumbersome is your annual meeting? Is there any way to reduce the associated tribulation?

Feature: Fierce Commitment to Sustaining and Helping the Community.

Reason: The 'Employees' and 'Managers' live here, it is their community, they see and recognize the problems that abound. Also in many cases they are aware of the individuals and/or families who request assistance from the Thrift Shop, but there is an unwritten understanding that there will not be any public discussion concerning those who make requests.

Consequence: There is great willingness to give of time and effort in the most beneficial manor.

Post Script – Larger Corporate Implications: How many employees are truly dedicated to the corporation they work for??

Question: How many of your employees are just there for the pay check, the recognition, the potential status advancement or any other none productive reasons? Give me a percentage, I would wager less than 10% and that 10% are upper management. Is there any sense that your business endeavors really benefit the community?

Feature: A Consciousness That 'I Work For A Larger Good'.

Reason: As stated above it is their community and they see the issues, problems and concerns.

Consequence: Dedication and Commitment.

Post Script – Larger Corporate Implications: How many employees in the corporate world see a greater 'good' in what they do? Aren't banks and brokerage firms really supporting the motivation of 'Greed." (This is not going to sit well!!) In actuality aren't all firms except benevolent social institutions really just fulfilling mankind's greed motivation? If this is the case any employee of any firm with any sort of conscience is to some degree having daily emotional confrontation. Now this of course leads to much larger issues, for motivation by 'Greed' also leads to greater competition among employees. Those who quest for position, power and greater retribution will work harder and longer! Are there only two primary motivational functions, 'Greed' or 'Serving the Greater Good? A much larger discussion can be presented here. But in the Thrift Shop there is the burning desire to serve the community, and the 'employees' and 'managers' are motivated accordingly.

Question: Do your employees see a greater 'good' in what they are doing?

Feature: 'Employees' are not paid.

Reason: The Thrift Shop has been a voluntary activity since initiation and those who assist understand this and look upon their time as a service to the community. There is a minimal compensation to the two managers and the treasurer, but this is generally acceptable to the rest of the staff.

Consequence: The usual ongoing jealousy and jockeying for position and status that is prevalent in the corporate world is not found.

Post Script – Larger Corporate Implications: From the perspective of the Corporate world salary, position, status, power and prestige can be viewed from two perspectives. In a positive sense this hopefully will lead to the employees working harder, seeking better knowledge and opportunities for advancement. From the negative perspective there is always to be found the issues of salary and appropriate compensation for work effort extended. There are always the discussions in the corner about salary, work accomplished etc. Once I found myself extremely irritated to say the least when I learned that my boss made 20% more but did less than half of the real work of the corporation. From that point on I had much less respect for the firm and perhaps became a bit less dedicated to my own position. Every firm has a very defined policy that salaries are not to be discussed or alluded to, really now? For further reference on this subject please see the Salary Review section of 'Up the Organization' by Robert Townsend.

Question: Do your employees appreciate theirs and the management's salary structure? What is the differentiation between the compensation for the CEO and Senior Management and the 'line' workers?

Feature: The Work Undertaken Involves Physical Movement.

Reason: Items that are donated need to be assessed, sorted, priced, and placed appropriately on the display shelves. There is the need for everyone to get up and walk about the building on a continual ongoing basis.

Consequence: People are not bound to a particular location and are not caught in a stationary position for endless hours.

Post Script – Larger Corporate Implications: Workers in the corporate environment are often sequestered at their work stations, cubicles, or offices staring at their computer screen for hours on end. There are obvious consequences; health issues, boredom, pent up energy and emotions etc. What is even worse is when the work station, cubicle, or office does not have a window access, which for many employees such as myself is a devastating consequence. A quick side note; in the most significant corporate engagement as a First VP personal responsibilities allowed 'travels' throughout the building as well as to other outside locations. This of course made the engagement much less destructive.

Question: Are you employees trapped in their little boxes without many options for physical movement?

Feature: Individuals Have the Need to Talk to Each Other and Discuss the Items that are being put up for sale.

Reason: Clothes, Knick Knacks, Housewares etc. have to be evaluated and mutual consensus is extremely valuable in the pricing and placement endeavors.

Consequence: There is the freedom of interaction and discussion giving the 'employees' a feeling of community, fellowship and friendship.

Post Script – Larger Corporate Implications: If only such opportunities could be afforded in the corporate environment. The only exchange of thoughts and ideas takes place in scheduled, disciplined meetings, were wording has to be cautiously set forth. Heaven forbid that you might have a personal phone call in your work cubicle, especially those cubicles with the lower walls. No privacy, no interpersonal discussion, you just can't try to be human in the corporate work environment.

Question: Obvious, how dehumanizing is your work environment?

Feature: Defined Work Hours.

Reason: The Thrift Shop is only open from 10 to 3 on week days, 10 to 4 on Saturdays and closed on Sundays.

Consequence: You know what time you will go in and what time you will be leaving and thus there is structure to your life with freedom to plan other events.

Post Script – Larger Corporate Implications: I would venture to say that there is no Corporation in today's world that does not expect employees to put in many more hours than the 'stated' work day. A quick personal event from the past: In one previous position from time to time there was the requirement to report to the work location during odd times of the night. One night at about 2:00 a.m. while walking from the Subway to the building it was necessary to pass garbage cans that had been put out for collection. Unfortunately there were about a dozen rats who were inhabiting those cans and hearing my presence they scurried across my feet to get to the street. Am surprised to this day that I was not bitten by one of the startled creatures. In the current corporate environment employees know that extra hours are required in order to keep their position and to be potentially considered for advancement so thus they put in the extra hours accordingly. Family, Social Activities, Community Commitments, are you serious? Burn out those employees, there are dozens if not hundreds graduating from business school each year.

Question: What are the real work hours of your firm? Do the employees appreciate and respect these hours or do they adhere to maintain status and position?

Feature: Do Not Have to Worry About the 'Bottom Line'.

Reason: Whatever extra resources the Thrift Shop has after paying upkeep is given to the needs of the community. Unfortunately there is always additional help that might be given, but funds are only distributed as available.

Consequence: The associates do not feel threaten by a corporate economy, but can extend themselves in the work as they feel fit and thus quite often give more generously of their time.

Post Script – Larger Corporate Implications: In the major corporate environment employees are encouraged to be aware of the balance sheet so that they will be induced to work harder and longer accordingly. In a difficult economy this quickly wears thin, as does the motivation. People wear out!! But there are always those new business school graduates. Said that before didn't I, am I getting the point across??

Question: How threatening is the 'Bottom Line' your employees?

Feature: Thrift Shop Associates are Local Residents.

Reason: All those who work with the Thrift Shop are within a very reasonable distance and are able to 'commute' easily.

Consequence: Excessive time is not consumed in traveling to and from work each day.

Post Script – Larger Corporate Implications: I defy you to find me a corporation where employees have less than an hour commute. Employees are exhausted before they even begin work. Difficult issue, many attempts have been made to remedy, but every time a corporation relocates to a 'better' site the environment becomes desirable for other corporate headquarters and affordable decent housing is even further out in the suburbs. Travel down route 110 on Long Island or visit Westchester County NY.

Question: On average how far and how long is the commute for the majority of your employees? (Note, as I remember there is almost no one who works in New York City who does not spend at least two hours a day commuting)

Feature: No Commuter Fees

Reason: Even though the volunteers at the Thrift Shop live within a short distance of the shop there are also reimbursed for travel costs on a monthly basis by a Sullivan County Organization that rewards volunteer workers.

Consequence: There is greater satisfaction in fulfilling the everyday endeavors knowing that there will be some compensation for the cost of traveling to and from the Shop. For some of the 'employees' this is of great benefit, for in the current economy for many of the associates expenses are carefully monitored.

Post Script – Larger Corporate Implications: The monthly commuter ticket from Mineola to Penn Station, (a short and rather reasonable commute that I use to take on a daily basis) is now $223 and the subway fare is $2.25 one way, and thus is $4.50 per day or $90 +/- a month. There are literally hundreds of thousands who commute from greater distances at much greater costs. This is of course another discouraging feature of the corporate work environment. These monthly fees do not serve to create a dedicated work force.

Question: What is the cost of the commute for your employees?

Feature: Formal Attire not requirement, in fact would be completely out of place.

Reason: The Thrift Shop is a laid back environment and the appropriate attire is beyond 'country casual' in fact most likely we give new definition to 'country casual'. Obviously everyone seeks to look decent enough and truth be known most the clothes that I wear when I serve in the Thrift Shop came from there. It is such a delight to wear shorts while waiting on customers.

Consequence: Great savings in the expense for clothes, shoes, ties, suits etc. There also is no subtle competition to look better than an associate.

Post Script – Larger Corporate Implications: In many of the corporate environments there are very significant requirements to be in business formal daily, and heaven forbid if a women wears the same dress two days in a row, or if a man wears the same shirt and tie two days in a row. A firm might have business casual Fridays, but that present issues in and of its self. Suits, ties, dress shoes become tiresome quite quickly but is a part of the corporate culture and must be tolerated. Formal business attire reaches a point wherein it is tolerated but not really appreciated.

Question: What are the attire standards and can they be mitigated?

Feature: Employees at any time have freedom to discuss objectives and make recommendation for change and innovation.

Reason: Basically most of the 'Leaders' and 'Employees' are friends and freely communicate with each other.

Consequence: Because of interpersonal relationships there has always been an open forum for recommendations etc.

Post Script – Larger Corporate Implications: Personal experience has been that very seldom do employees in the corporate environment experience a sense of friendship, but most see themselves in competition with each other and with management. In fact look

ing back the only time that employees had the potential to consider innovations was during the yearly review when the goals for the coming year were grudgingly delineated.

Question: Is there the freedom for open discussions between 'employees' and 'management'. This also raises the issue of whether there is such a severe differentiation between the 'employees' and 'management' that employees are afraid to step out of their predefined boxes? What is a cubicle anyway?

Feature: Thrift Store Stock is Free and Delivered

Reason: People bring items to the Thrift Store, the items to do not have to be purchased or picked up.

Consequence: There are no problems or issues of Vendor Management.

Post Script – Larger Corporate Implications: Now a moment for true confessions. In one position in the corporate world I was responsible for Vendor Management and enjoyed this role tremendously in that it involved expensive lunches, trips, and assessments of the operations of various endeavors. There was even a trip one year to Las Vegas for a postal convention. Life was good! But of course there was the other aspect that I was the one held accountable if product was not delivered on a timely basis and was not within specifications.

Question: How much time and resources in your firm is spent on Vendor Management? Are there ways in which this can be better effectuated?

Postscript: Unfortunately all of the concerns for the Thrift Shop may be for naught in that being at the mercy of the owner who is leasing us the space we may be subject to eviction at any time. He has quite pointedly made it known to us that he could lease out our space for a much better return. We have sought diligently to maintain a good relationship with the owner, but he does hold this threat over our heads. Since we could not afford to pay a greater amount of rent and be effectual in the community and since there are no other facilities available this would mean the ending of the Thrift shop endeavors.

Some Further Notes: Having been a business consultant in the past years would consider engagements to assess the human/personnel issues that are inhibiting work endeavors within your firm. As mentioned initially am seeking response to this presentation and would invite written commentary at the e-mail address: **TheNewEndeavor@Gmail.com**. I will seek to assess these comments and provide some form of response accordingly, perhaps another written endeavor, or an extensive evolving web page.

www.ingramcontent.com/pod-product-compliance
Lightning Source LLC
LaVergne TN
LVHW010945110826
845149LV00013B/2765

* 9 7 8 0 9 8 8 8 5 4 9 0 1 *